Ghosts of the
Graham Mansion

Also about the Graham Mansion by Thomas D. Perry

The Graham Mansion: A History and Guide

Stranger Than Fiction: Reid Stanger Fulton of the Graham Mansion

Several excerpts from this book are included in this text.

See all Thomas D. Perry's publications at

www.freestateofpatrick.com

Ghosts of the Graham Mansion

By Thomas D. Perry

ISBN-13: 978-1466493087

ISBN-10: 1466493089

Laurel Hill Publishing

P. O. Box 11

4443 Ararat Highway

Ararat, Virginia 24053

www.freestateofpatrick.com

freestateofpatrick@yahoo.com

276-692-5300

For J. E. B. Stuart,

whose spirit first brought me to the Graham Mansion

"All that we see or seem is but a dream within a dream."

Edgar Allan Poe

Quotes from this author are throughout this book.

Contents

At a Court of Oyer & Terminer held at the Court House of Montgomery County the 5 day of May 1786 for the tryal of Bob & Sam two negro... Slaves ... killing & murdering Joseph Baker there present. James McGavock, Andrew Boyd, Robt Sayers, Adam Dean, ... & John T. Sayers Gent.

The above named Bob & Sam being brought to the Bar in custody... it was demanded of them whither they were guilty of said crime or not they answ'd & said there were... but examination of the s'd Bob & Sam they confesed there were guilty of said charge in consideration of which the Court are of opinion that they are guilty of the fact wherewith they stand charg'd & that they be... according to Law on Tuesday the 16th Instant. whereupon the Court proceded to value Bob at £120 & Sam at £80. The Court... arise. James McGavock.

At a Court held in Montgomery County the 23 day of May 1786.
Present. Andrew Boyd, Adam Dean, Robert Sayers & Daniel Howe Gent.

A deed of Bargain & Sale from Benjamin Clements to John Harding proved by these oaths William Calfee, James Calfee & Richard Ellis three of the witnesses thereto ₰ O. R.

Court trial from the Montgomery County Virginia
Courthouse of the slaves Bob and Sam.

Foreword

"Coincidences, in general, are great stumbling blocks in the way of that class of thinkers who have been educated to know nothing of the theory of probabilities- that theory to which the most glorious objects of human research are indebted for the most glorious of illustration."

I came to this project a skeptic, but I was the only one. Everyone whether a paranormal investigator or just a tourist looking for a scare at the annual haunted house leaves the Graham Mansion in Wythe County, Virginia, with an eerie feeling. While I never personally experienced anything within the confines of the palatial home along the New River, I did once have an experience.

In the summer of 1999, after a divorce and in the middle of a relationship with a female reenactor in northern Virginia, I found myself alone in her farmhouse in the upstairs bedroom. She told me there was a spirit in the room, but I dismissed that as just weird. I found out that summer day in broad daylight with no thought of ghosts or spirits running through my mind. When suddenly in the guest bedroom as I started to exit I felt COLD envelop me and the hairs on the back of my neck stood straight up. I got out of that room in a hurry and never experienced anything again in the house.

After writing a history of the Graham Mansion in 2011, I saw the market for a book about the paranormal experiences at the house. Am I still a skeptic? Well, you will have to read this book and see!

--Tom Perry, November 4, 2011.

Confederate Regimental Flag of Major David Graham's 51st Virginia Infantry.

Chapter One

The Woman in the Window

"The death of a beautiful woman, is unquestionably the most poetical topic in the world."

The Graham Mansion and slave quarters to the left.

On Tuesday, February 24, 1864, a woman stood in the window staring out across the countryside of Southwest Virginia's Wythe County. She looked northeast towards the family cemetery on the high hill opposite the massive mansion that was only a decade old that day.

That late winter day, Civil War ravaged the two countries that were the United States and the Confederate States of America. In northern Georgia, Virginia born Union General George Thomas attacked Virginia born Joseph

Johnston near Dalton. At the Battle of Tunnel Hill or Buzzard's Roost, Georgia, the Confederates repulsed the Yankees that day, but learned a lesson not to attack head on the Southern positions that defended Atlanta. A lesson that Union General William T. Sherman used to his advantage later that year when he took Atlanta, then marched to the sea, and took Savannah by Christmas 1864.

In Washington, D. C., United States President Lincoln signed a bill passed by Congress that offered up to $300 compensation for any Union master whose slaves volunteered to join the Army. The bill freed the slaves at the end of his service. The act also offered increased compensation for volunteers, increased penalties for draft resistance, allowed Blacks to be subject to the draft, and ordered alternative service in non-combat roles for those who would not bear arms for religious reasons.

In Nevada Territory that same day, Virginia City Territorial Enterprise reporter Samuel Clemens wrote about a possible gold discovery near the Truckee River about fifteen miles away. Clemens was not yet Mark Twain.

The woman in the window carved into the window with a diamond ring the date, but who was she. Many ghost hunters claimed to hear the "What's your name?" during their investigations. There are many theories as to the identity of the woman and a good mystery to solve as this book tells about the people and the spirits that lived and may still haunt the Graham Mansion in Max Meadows, Wythe County, Virginia.

The window survives to this day with multiple initials carved with only one name, Mary Bell Peirce. The initials include MBP, MBG, EPP, BAG (beside the date of February 24, 1864,), and ECR. History might tell us that initials stand for Mary Bell Peirce, Mary Bell Graham, Elizabeth Pannill Peirce and Bettie Ann Graham, and Elizabeth C Robinson.

Tradition tells us that young women often carved their initials into a window in the childhood home to test the worth of their fiancé to see if the diamond in their engagement rings were real or fake. It is possible that these initials were carved the same day, possibly February 24, 1864, as the handwriting looks similar. We will never know for sure, but it gives us several directions to go.

One theory is that Mary Bell Peirce the niece of Martha Peirce Graham wrote her name in the window. She was the daughter of James and Nancy Ann Stuart Peirce, the latter was the older sister of Civil War General James Ewell Brown "Jeb" Stuart. Mary Bell was also the niece of Martha Peirce Graham, the wife of Squire David Graham and sister of James Peirce. Squire David and Martha owned the massive mansion with the carved window.

Mary Bell Peirce married Dr. James Magill. This is the happier version of the story, but not all stories end happily ever after.

Chapter Two

A Haunted House

"It is by no means an irrational fancy that, in a future

existence, we shall look upon what we think our present

existence, as a dream."

In the mid-1990s, a woman from Baltimore and her
aunt found themselves riding around the back roads of
Wythe County, Virginia. Her aunt described a local old
house as the "Vampire House." Intrigued, she found the
house that "took her breath away." While leaning against
the gate, she discovered it was unlocked. She quickly
moved up the hill to take photos. Two days later, she

returned to find a "caretaker," who told her he had "seen things."

In 2002 in Volume Seven of his *The Ghosts of Virginia,* author L. B. Taylor in Chapter 47 titled "The Haunted House That Looks Like A Haunted House" talks of the Graham Mansion. Truer words were never written. From the first time I (Tom Perry) saw the mansion in the 1980s, I thought "Haunted House." Actually, I think I started humming the theme to Scooby Doo Where Are You? the cartoon television show of my youth.

Each fall the Graham Mansion becomes a "Haunted House" as Spooky World USA turns it into a place for a scare during October culminating at Halloween. Paranormal Investigators say this action stirs up activity in the nearly two-hundred-year-old home.

Taylor describes several stories about the Graham Mansion and the "haints" that live there. Called a "Valley of Contention and Strife" because of the feuds between neighbors, the home also referred to as the "Vampire House," sits in an out of the way location now along

Virginia Route 619. Once though it was the "back way" between Pulaski's Draper Valley and Wytheville for many such as future Civil War General James Ewell Brown "Jeb" Stuart.

Taylor describes the visit to the mansion by Dorothy Brigandi of Baltimore, Maryland, in the mid-1990s, who had a surprise in her photos when she returned home. One had a "white mass," and she did not use a flash. Another had a "man" standing inside looking outside a window. He was "bald-headed, with his right arm across his chest and what looks like a silver band on his wrist." She describes a woman "sitting in the corner under his hand wearing possibly a black wrap." Dorothy told Taylor a "spirit reader" said there were "four spirits" in the house and the feeling of torture and pain in the slave quarters.

Taylor told of his visit to the "rather creepy" Graham Mansion describing it as right out of Alfred Hitchcock's movie *Psycho*. He speaks of his interview and conversation with local newspaperwoman Linda Spiker, who said of Dorothy's photos, "If you are looking for a ghost, you may discern the likely shape of two, and perhaps three figures that appear to be looking out the window."

Whether it is a "Haunted House" as Taylor and I perceived or as the "greatest house I have ever seen," the Graham Mansion certainly attracts some eccentric owners and some curious visitors who may encounter some strange spirits any time of the year.

The original section of the Graham Mansion.

Chapter Three

Emancipation

"I was never kinder to the old man than during the whole week before I killed him."

Image believed to be Joseph Baker.

Some of the spirits in and around the Graham Mansion remind us of the dark side of American History. Whether it is the cruelty of slavery or the action of vigilante justice, the house in Max Meadows has seen it all.

During the American Revolution in 1777, the area around the Graham Mansion became Montgomery County. In 1779, George Shillideay sold 198 acres to Joseph Baker along Cedar Run. Many local historians report that the frame section of the Graham Mansion was built around the 1785 log cabin owned by Joseph Baker.

The local story has it that Joseph Baker and two of his slaves, Bob and Sam, were making moonshine "out back." Baker told the slaves that in his will he would give them their freedom upon his death. The slaves hastened Baker's untimely demise..." Whether drinking or an argument or both along with the promise of freedom through murder caused the assault is not known, but often suspected.

In the Montgomery Courthouse, there is a record of the sheriff arresting Bob and Sam, their subsequent trial, and their hanging. There is also a record of the sheriff being paid 200 lbs. of tobacco for his efforts in 1786.

Local lore has it that Bob and Sam's spirits "still roam the hills surrounding Cedar Run." One tradition has the Sheriff hung Bob and Sam from a hickory tree on the hill overlooking the mansion and buried the slaves there, but according to court documents they were "probably" hung at Fort Chiswell, and their burial place is unknown.

John Baker inherited the land on which the Graham Mansion sits today. Other records show that in 1787 James and Rebecca Tuttle moved to Wilkes County, Georgia, and sold 400 acres to John Baker. This land became Wythe County in 1790 named for the mentor of Thomas Jefferson, George Wythe, who also died a horrible death poisoned with arsenic possibly by his nephew.

In 1793, Baker sold 187 acres to Daniel Miller. The property came to the Crockett family next, and from them, the land along Cedar Run came to the Grahams. The Graham family owned slaves too for three decades from the mid-1820s until the end of the Civil War in 1865. In 1860, Graham employed 29 slaves of his own and hired dozens more from other owners to operate his many operations. Slave labor supported the Southern agricultural economy, but also the industrial economy of the region. The Small

Special Collections Library at the University of Virginia houses the papers on the Graham, Tate, and Sanders families containing twenty ledger books and over 3,000 papers documenting the business interests of Squire and Major David Graham including books on their slaves. In June 1830, as an example, the "Slave Book" lists the names of those held in bondage as Carter, Charles, Isaac, Phil, Duke, Dennis, Jack, Will, Buck, Terry, Caesar, Randal, George, Ben, Lewis, Sam, Peter, Adam, Rueben, Matt, Bryer, Church, Terry, Hardin and Bill. Many persons with clairvoyant abilities talk about the slaves and one in particular named Bob.

Chapter Four

Squire

"Men have called me mad; but the question is not yet settled, whether madness is or is not the loftiest intelligence– whether much that is glorious– whether all that is profound– does not spring from disease of thought– from moods of mind exalted at the expense of the general intellect."

One of the darker spirits inhabiting the Graham Mansion is Squire David Graham, the original builder of the house. Descending from an Irish lineage, David Graham, the man we call "Squire" was born on September 3, 1800. His father, Robert, died when he was 10 or 11 years old.

At age 26, Squire David purchased 2000 acres in twelve tracts, various iron-making buildings, and a furnace on Reed Creek and Cedar Run from the Crockett heirs (James and Andrew) and John Baker for $10,000. This purchase included a 213-acre tract on Cedar Run on what today most people call the Major David Graham Mansion, but it is misnamed. It should be called the Squire David Graham Mansion in honor of the Major's father. For this book, we refer to it as the Graham Mansion as the house is really a building built by father and son with the same name.

Squire David built the original house and the majority of the later additions. The original, rear wooden frame section of the Mansion was built in the 1830s possibly around the log structure of the Bakers, and the large, formal brick section was added in the 1850s.

The Graham Mansion was built in four stages, two under the direction of Squire David Graham (1838 and 1855) and two under his son's direction (1870 and 1890). In 1848, bricks made locally went into another significant

Mansion "addition." By 1855-56, another major Mansion "addition" included a 45 foot square by the 40-foot high brick structure. We know this because there is a substantial increase in value on property tax paid in 1840, which indicates additions to the large building.

Squire David Graham was a big part of his community for several decades. He was a Justice of the Peace in 1826. That same year he acquired a "license for a house of private entertainment." He was a Trustee of Methodist Brick Church in 1837 as his wife was a Methodist. He was Presbyterian and founded Galena Presbyterian Church in 1850. He even managed to get his face on a $10 bill from the South Western Bank of Wytheville.

By 1860, Squire David Graham accumulated 6,000 acres of land. His "real property" was worth $70,000 and included as many as fourteen iron furnaces along with forges, gristmills, rolling mills, nail works, and even a general store.

Graham, known as the "first ironsmith of southwest Virginia," was part owner of the nearby Wythe Union Lead Mines, which he purchased for $8,000 in 1853 from William and Alexander Peirce including 1,400 acres. Graham was a Director of the Virginia and Tennessee Railroad. Squire David Graham built an iron furnace just down the road from the Mansion. Pig iron from the Graham forges went by horse-drawn wagon to larger cities and tradition states then it went overseas to England.

He produced iron products such as large salt kettles for the saltworks in Saltville, stoves, nails, plates, pipes, rails, hobbles for horses, firebacks, and iron for cannons for at least forty-four years and possibly fifty years.

Squire David Graham lived until 1870, but the last ten years of his life were caught up in the great conflagration that was war. Whether you call it Civil War or the War Between the States, the "great scourge of war" affected his life and that of his children in ways, they could not have imagined in 1860.

Squire David Graham wrote his will on February 8, 1870. In the document, he left 3,600 acres to his son David, 1,700 acres to daughter Elizabeth Robinson, 818 acres to daughter Mary Matthews and 1,500 acres to daughter Emily. He divided his interest in the lead mines with 1/3 to his son and the remaining 2/3 to his daughters collectively.

When Squire David Graham passed on October 16, 1870, at Cedar Run Farm, the Wytheville Dispatch had this to say about him. "The whole country and district of Southwest Virginia will feel affected with this information, as he was so well and so favorably known. The name of David Graham was in all the public enterprises of the district, in which he took a large and lively interest. His advice, his skill, and his experience were sought on almost every occasion of importance, and his counsels were widely beneficial to his neighbors and his friends. In his own proper department of industry, he had no compeer (a person of equal status) in the district. He commanded the greatest success, producing the best material, and his brand of iron is so generally known and sought after, that he realized for it the highest market price from season to season. He had correct knowledge of the quality and value of ores, and his selection of them proved his sound experience. He was distinguished by thoughtful action, by true friendship, and by Christian integrity, and there is in his case a certain hope of resurrection until life eternal. A very large concourse attended his funeral and attested the high esteem in which he was held. May he ever rest in peace."

It appears that Squire David Graham did rest in peace. One investigator reported the following. "I have had many experiences with someone coming up behind me and growling in my ear. When I turn to see who it is there is never anyone there. And often, I have been standing in the corner of a room or up against a wall. Kind of hard for someone to sneak up and growl directly in your ear like that when you're in such a position. As I understand it, there are those who believe this to be Squire."

Chapter Five

Martha

"I became insane, with long intervals of horrible sanity."

Martha Peirce Graham is a mysterious figure. The wife of Squire David and mother of Major David Peirce Graham suffered from mental illness documented in her daughter Elizabeth's journal from just before and during the first few years of the Civil War.

In the two months since arriving home from Philadelphia, Bettie Graham continued to keep her journal. She wrote on May 7, 1861. "Ma does not seem to be in her right mind at all today. She takes up the strangest ideas I have ever heard of; she's got it into her head that Cousin Laura is a rogue and steals all her eggs, brandy and sugar, and that she is going to have a child. Poor Cousin Laura! She is so innocent and unsuspecting." Two days later she wrote, "Cousin Bell is coming down next week; I never wanted to see anybody so badly in my life as I do her for I love her oh! so dearly." This is probably Mary Bell Peirce, the niece of J. E. B. Stuart and daughter of James and Nancy Anne Dabney Stuart Peirce. Mary Bell Peirce's signature is carved into the upstairs bedroom in the Graham Mansion.

At the Graham Mansion in October 1861, Bettie noted her mother's continuing erratic behavior. On the 9th, "Ma has been cutting up terribly this morning, saying we would disgrace ourselves." The next day she noted, "I promised Willie I wouldn't smoke anymore, so I have given all my segars away to Bell Peirce. I have quit whistling also, under promise to the same personage."

There is evidence that Squire David Graham imprisoned his wife in a basement room. "Her signature can be found on one of the basement shackle room doors, where it is believed she was locked away when guests came to visit the family." Martha Peirce Graham died on October 22, 1865, during the war. Such was the sad ending for the mistress of the Graham mansion.

Squire David Graham married Martha Bell Peirce of nearby Poplar Camp, Virginia, on December 15, 1835. Born on February 2, 1806, she was the daughter of David and Mary Bell Peirce. They lived first at Boiling Springs, where they buried two infants before he brought her to the "Cedar Run Farm." Their "often stormy union" produced many children, although two died as infants as previously stated before 1837.

The couple had five surviving children. David Graham (1838-1898) married Nannie Montgomery Tate, the daughter of Charles Campbell Tate and Elizabeth Friel. Major David Graham, the firstborn surviving child, served in the War Between the States and inherited the mansion from his father, Squire David Graham. Robert Calving Graham (1841-1852) died young. Mary Bell Graham (1843-1900) married H. J. Matthews. Elizabeth Ann Graham (1845-1921) married John W. Robinson, who became a business partner with his brother-in-law, Major David Graham. Emily Maria Graham (1848-1889) married J. W. McGavock and was the last child of Martha and Squire David Graham.

Many paranormal investigators and clairvoyants believe Martha to be a tortured spirit just as she was in life. In the window described at the beginning of this book was Martha the M. Bell Peirce as her name was Martha Bell Peirce Graham. Did she carve her maiden name in the glass along with the female members of her family during a time of bliss while her mind fought reality? We will never know for sure, but there is little doubt that Martha did not live a happy life in the mansion her husband and son built.

Stone used to step up to mount a horse.

Chapter Six

What's Your Name, Little Girl?

"The most natural, and, consequently, the truest and most intense of the human affections are those which arise in the heart as if by electric sympathy."

The rear second-floor bedroom of the Graham Mansion is the site of Bettie Graham's Civil War era schoolroom. This is also the room that a "clairvoyant" encountered "Clara," an orphan from the time of the Civil War, who Emily and Bettie Graham, daughters of Squire David and Martha Graham kept and tutored her with the other children. When Squire David Graham discovered the presence of "Clara" he strongly disapproved, but the girl died of tuberculosis or pneumonia. There is no paper trail for Clara in the census, or other documentation and her name may not be Clara, but she is a spirit that does not like men, possibly from the relationship with Squire David, but much paranormal activity occurs in the room that bears her name.

On one of the first paranormal investigations at the mansion in 2007, a voice asks, "What's your name?" just like present owner Josiah Cephas Weaver might sing the cover of the Lynyrd Skynyrd song "What's your name, little girl? What's your name?" The little girl's name is Clara. Other investigators report hearing footsteps on the stairs outside her room in the oldest section of the house.

Another investigation placed a plasma ball in the middle of the room to attract a response to the light and the energy that it creates. One investigator noticed "a strange fainted white light in almost a square shape. It was moving very fast and floating above the plasma ball. The light moved to the floor up the wall around the ceiling and halfway around the room before it disappeared moving very fast at times and slow to the point of floating." Two investigators witnessed the occurrence. The room was swept a K-2 meter to see if any electromagnetic field were present. None were found, or cold spots felt. No outside light from flashlights or passing car lights were detected, and all investigators were in their locations. The only other members in the house were watching camera monitors. No one saw anything.

In Clara's room, another investigation involved a female in the closet doing an EVP session when she asked, "Is there anyone in here with me?" she got an "immediate Class A response of "I'm in here with you!" Apparently, there was also some interest in the attractiveness of the investigator commenting on her anatomy.

In October of 2009, one investigator reported the following. "My daughter and I both saw a little girl standing in front of a door and quickly turn to go further into the room. By the time, we were able to see where she went she had hidden in the closet on the right side of the room and was peaking out at us. Just as quickly, she disappeared.

My daughter said she told her to, 'come here.' I didn't hear

that, but we BOTH saw her."

Chapter Seven

Ghosts of the Graham Mansion

Jonathan

"Years of love have been forgot, In the hatred of a minute."

One of the more playful spirits encountered at the Graham Mansion is a young slave named Jonathan. The legend is that Squire David Graham hung the boy for stealing something.

Jonathan is known for running through the house with "Big Footsteps" chasing after him. EVPs have revealed a voice saying, "Help, he is after me."

Shadows

"The boundaries which divide Life from Death are at best shadowy and vague. Who shall say where the one ends, and where the other begins?"

One paranormal investigator was in Clara's room on the second floor "classroom." When they looked towards the doorway after hearing something outside the entrance, they saw a "shadow of a person – the head and shoulders" that gave them chills. Upon investigation, no one was seen, and no one was on the second floor at the time.

The Bride

"Beauty of whatever kind, in its supreme development, invariably excites the sensitive soul to tears."

A clairvoyant claimed a woman that is described as the "women in white" looks out the window of a room on the second floor known as the "Bride's Room." This same clairvoyant reported the woman is wearing a wedding dress. Some speculate she is waiting for her fiancé that may have died during the Civil War.

Another related story involves the overseer's house that you can see from the "Bride's Room." Recently, the man of the house claimed to see a woman in white waiting for him at the bottom of the home's steps inside, but his wife never saw the apparition. Could it be she is searching for a long lost man in both houses?

A paranormal investigation heard knocking from the adjoining room (Christmas Room), and it repeated its self on a couple of occasions. No one else was in the house at the time. The sound stopped and when the two investigators left the room and one experienced "chill bumps" and his hair stood straight up on his right arm. "He said he felt as if someone walked right past him to go into the room."

Gracie

"Yes, I now feel that it was then on that evening of sweet dreams- that the very first dawn of human love burst upon the icy night of my spirit. Since that period I have never seen nor heard your name without a shiver half of delight, half of anxiety."

One investigator believed he pieced "together a rather compelling story." He elaborated, "Whether it was the one of who we believe to be Martha Graham in the basement saying, 'Can You Please Tell Gracie...I Need Her,' or the sound of a little girl whispering 'hide'...the story only starts there." He believes that one of the Graham men possibly Squire David Graham still "rules over the house with an iron fist."

An EVP (Electronic Voice Phenomenon) captured in the Music Room during an investigation. This particular room has a piano. An investigator sang the old traditional hymn, *Amazing Grace*, stopping in mid-verse to see if something will finish the tune. When recordings were reviewed, a woman's voice was singing "*da da daa da.*"

General Store

"Science has not yet taught us if madness is or is not the sublimity of the intelligence."

With many outbuildings surrounding the Graham Mansion, the search for ghosts has expanded to them as well. The General Store, once a barn on the property is one of these structures.

During one investigation, a male and female pair found themselves alone in the building doing EVP work, when the female felt something touch her ankle. They used a flashlight and a K-2 meter and found nothing. He placed the meter at the female's feet when she again felt something touch her ankle, but no change on the meter.

On another occasion, three male investigators in the General Store doing EVP work asked a question about Jeffersonville, now Tazewell, and received a growling response. All three heard the response. They asked the question, "So I take it you don't like the town?" Another growling response. The investigator went outside to check the building perimeter and found nothing.

One investigator reported the following. "In the attic of the general store, I get very disoriented and sick to my stomach. It almost feels like barometric pressure, but not quite. It's a very heavy and painful feeling."

Shackles

"Deep into that darkness peering, long I stood there, wondering, fearing, doubting, dreaming dreams no mortal ever dared to dream before."

One paranormal group filmed a figure at the back door to the outside walking by the door. A few minutes later, an orb is seen for just a moment at the same entrance.

The Shackle Room in the basement is a place of much dark legend as Squire David Graham reportedly kept his mentally ill wife, Martha, locked in the room. There are names carved on the inner wall of the door to the room.

With the institution of slavery being present in the South during the first thirty years of the time the Grahams lived in the mansion, there is little doubt that slaves were punished with time in the room.

The Graves of Squire David and Martha Peirce Graham.

Chapter Eight

Confederates In The Attic

(Includes Excerpts from

The Graham Mansion: A History and Guide)

"In our endeavors to recall to memory something long forgotten, we often find ourselves upon the very verge of remembrance, without being able, in the end, to remember."

On the third floor of the Graham Mansion is an attic room that tradition holds was a meeting place for Confederates during the War Between the States. Major David Graham, son of Squire David and Martha Graham, was an officer in the 51st Virginia Infantry. His sister, Bettie's, diary from the war often speaks of her brother and other Confederate officers being present at the house during the war.

One female investigator told of an experience while doing EVP work with another woman. "We were both sitting on the floor on the right side of the room (as you're entering the room on the right side). We were asking questions when

I suddenly felt a chilly breeze on the left side of my body." She asked the other lady "if she felt a breeze. She did not." The two began asking questions again, and the original investigator once again felt this same breeze along with her left side. She asked direct questions "about this chilly breeze." She seemed to get a response with another chilly breeze at my side. We resumed our questioning and felt the breeze one last time. The other investigator did not feel a breeze in the room. The room is very stuffy being on the top of the house with no open windows. They could not find a natural opening to explain the wind.

The winds of war came to the Graham Mansion in 1861. Company B of the 51st Virginia Infantry was from Wythe County under David Peirce Graham. Company B, the Wharton Grays, formerly Company H enlisted July 31, 1861, for one year. This unit joined the 51st Virginia Regiment on August 14, 1861. Grahams serving in the regiment were A. J., David Peirce, Jackson, James, Noah B., Parris M., and Zaccheus.

At Camp Jackson in Wytheville, the Grahams joined the companies of the 51st Regiment of Virginia Infantry under the command of an 1847 graduate of the Virginia Military Institute and civil engineer, Gabriel C. Wharton. Born in Culpeper, Virginia, Wharton graduated second in his class at the VMI. Practicing Civil Engineering in Arizona before the war, he became a major in the 45th Virginia in July 1861 and then Colonel of the 51st Virginia Infantry.

Joining the first commander, Colonel Gabriel C. Wharton, were the Field Officers of the 51st Virginia Infantry including Major William T. Akers, Major George A. Cunningham, Major Stephen M. Dickey, Lt. Colonel Augustus Forsberg, Major David P. Graham, Lt. Colonel James W. Massie, Lt. Colonel Samuel H. Reynolds, Lt. Colonel John P. Wolfe, and Major William A. Yonce.

Augustus Forsberg wrote of them at this time, "It was interesting to notice the personnel of the volunteer-like mountaineers, they were courageous, fine physical development, and could compare with any troops on earth...Some in uniforms they had made at home, some with squirrel rifles, some with flintlocks and Bowie knifes. Some had never seen a railroad. Once the sound of a locomotive was heard and the men acted like being shocked, one called out 'She's a coming', down went all guns and like a flock of sheep, ran down the hill to see the Iron Horse."

Born in Sweden in 1832, Forsberg served as a Swedish Army Engineer before coming to America in the 1850s. He rose in rank to Colonel and command of the 51st Virginia Infantry Regiment in 1863.

In August 1861, the regiment took the train to Bonsack Depot, just east of present-day Roanoke, and camped from August 5 until September 19. The regiment moved to the Kanawha Valley in present-day West Virginia in early September leaving the two Patrick companies behind.

The First Battle of Manassas occurred on July 21, 1861, with a rousing Southern victory and propelling Thomas J. Jackson to the legend of "Stonewall" Jackson. The reader will note that David P. Graham did not raise men until ten days after the battle continuing to be cautious that war might be avoided.

Next came a trip to Kentucky for the regiment. The journey to the "Bluegrass State" took eight days for the regiment. The men traveled via five railroads to Bristol, Knoxville, Chattanooga, Nashville, and Bowling Green. During the stay in Kentucky, Woolwine reported the death of General Felix Zollicoffer at the Battle of Mill Springs on January 17, 1862, and his first pay: "Here we drawed the first money we ever drawed from the time we come into the service." James I. Robertson quotes General Floyd on the 51st in 1862 saying, "They have not a single dollar to purchase the least little comfort, even for the sick."

U. S. Grant earned the moniker "Unconditional Surrender" when he forced the capitulation of Fort Henry and Fort Donelson. The 51st Virginia under the command of another VMI graduate, Colonel James W. Massie, fought in the thick at Fort Donelson in February 1862. This battle was a rugged baptism into the rigors of war for the young men.

On February 15, Wharton's Brigade attacked the Federal right and opened an escape route at the cost of 9 killed, 43 wounded and 5 missing. The sniping generals, Floyd and Pillow, failed to follow up the success of the breakout. The next day Floyd's command escaped before the surrender of the fort. The men made their way to Nashville, Chattanooga, and finally to Abingdon. Going into winter camp at Glade Spring, the wounded recuperated in the hospital at Emory and Henry College.

The 51st continued in Wharton's Brigade in the Army of the Kanawha and remained in the Department of Southwestern Virginia through the rest of 1862.

Wharton's brigade returned to Virginia in the spring of 1862 and occupied the Kanawha Valley the following September.

August Forsberg commented in his diary about the service of Major Graham. "The morning of the 10th (March 1862) I was lifted on my horse, and followed my regiment as long as I could do so mounted. Two o'clock P. M. was agreed upon by the Commanders for the attack in front &

rear, but our guide had taken us by such a route that when Gen. Williams commenced firing, we were yet some miles from the position assigned us. At the first report of the guns in front of town we were ordered to 'double quick.' In the excitement I forgot all about the pain in my wounded knee, dismounted and with aid of my sword, used as a walking cane, I hobbled along with my men. The weather was intensely hot and the men, being moved so rapidly over such rough ground, soon became exhausted and scattered. I reached the position in rear of town, with only a handful of men, just as a Federal wagon train was making its way out. It was fired into and forced to return. The enemy, observing his communications with the rear threatened, advanced most of his available Infantry to dislodge us from the ridge we occupied, and, assisted by a battery within easy range, he was not far from success. But for the stubborn defence made principally by Capt. Graham of the 51st and his company nearest to the road, the day may not have been ours. Until dark firing continued on both sides, without any advantage gained. During the night, the Feds

51

burned some of their stores, and evacuated the town successfully- I suppose very much to their own surprise. The engagement at Fayette C. H. was heralded as a great triumph to the Southern Army, but the fact that Col. Sieber with his inferior Federal force escaped unmolested during the night with his artillery and most of his trains, proves, I believe, his superior management, or great oversight on our part."

On March 11, David P. Graham came home on furlough from the war. Bettie noted it in her journal. Two weeks later, his stay was extended until May 1. On March 28, she wrote that her brother's horse hurt his arm. She wrote on April 6 that they were surprised by "the arrival of Captain Forsberg and Major Densy. They are going to church today." The next day, "The rain has kept the gentlemen with us today." The next day she played "Charity" on the piano for the visitors and "Captain Forsberg paid great attention and thought it very fine." The happy interlude ended on April 11 when the guests left, but they were back eleven days later. One wonders if the officers were interested in the charms of Miss Bettie Graham. It was a long way from Forsberg's Sweden to Wythe County, Virginia. Sensing this brother David would not allow her to give Forsberg a "needle case." She gave it to him anyway on April 27. On May 1, she noted a year passing since leaving Baltimore, Maryland, on the way home from Philadelphia. Forsberg was not the only man interested in Bettie Graham. Two days later she wrote, "Went to the Forge. I rode Wesley's horse and the girt broke and I fell off. Mr. Robinson came back with me in the buggy." Mr. Robinson was either her future father-in-law or future husband John Robinson, who was a partner with her brother David in business.

Bettie Graham continued to write about the home front in Wythe County visiting her brother David in Wytheville during May. "We were in Brother's tent and had refreshments consisting of dried huckleberries." She noted her brother was suffering from a boil on his back. She noted that there was some "beau hunting" going on writing, "As we were coming out of church some of the men who belonged to Otey's battery said, 'I wish some of these young ladies would ask me to go home with them.' We went on however without catching a beau until we got back to the bank, where were stationed Col. Wharton, Capt. Forsberg, Major Denessy and Lt. Tate. I walked on with the Capt. Nan came next with the Col. Mary with the Major and Lid with the Lieut. They staid until twelve o'clock. At night Mary A. took off her shoes and found her feet all swollen. We raised a great laugh on her about it, telling her that her feet swelled with the effort to catch a beau, and that she ran her feet off running after the beaux, etc."

In June 1862, William Hanson Tate wrote of the man who one day in the future would marry his sister, Nannie. "Captain Graham arrived late Saturday evening. We were much rejoiced to meet him. He is not looking well." David Peirce Graham like many men serving in the war experienced health problems caused by exposure to new diseases or the stress of the war and the responsibility of taking men into battles where the loss of life was extremely prevalent.

One of the principal objectives of the Union forces involved capturing the salt mines at Saltville and the lead mines in Wythe County. These threats required the Confederate government to keep troops in southwest Virginia to protect these sources. The mines were essential to the Confederate armies as a source of both salt and lead were in southwestern Virginia. In the spring of 1862, the 51st went to meet a Federal force that had captured Princeton, Virginia, now West Virginia. The regiment succeeded in driving the Federal troops from the nearly destroyed town.

A unit of the 51st under Captain William T. Akers traveled to White Sulphur Springs and lost to a stronger Federal force. Captain Akers and his troops escaped by burning a bridge behind them. In June 1862, the 51st returned to Giles County. Later that month, it encamped at Peterstown, now in West Virginia. On July 3, the unit assisted in defeating a Federal force at Mercer Courthouse. For the next several weeks, members of the 51st remained in camp near Narrows in Giles County.

In August 1862, General W. W. Loring assumed command of the Department of Southwestern Virginia. Wharton's Brigade (including the 51st and 50th Regiments and 23rd Battalion of Infantry along with Stamp's Artillery) moved into Monroe County and at Lewisburg on August 28 routed a Federal force led by future president Colonel Rutherford B. Hayes.

Threatened by a much larger Union army, Wharton returned to Narrows. The 51st Regiment, now under the command of Lieutenant Colonel Augustus Forsberg, moved to Grey Sulphur Springs where it drilled for several weeks and served on picket duty. In early September 1862, the brigade moved back into present-day West Virginia and defeated a Federal force at Montgomery Ferry on the Kanawha River. It captured a large number of supplies including food, clothing, and arms.

The Confederates again occupied Charleston, driving the Federal forces toward the Ohio River. They camped for several weeks, enjoying the luxury of the captured supplies. Loring decided to move from Charleston back to the

Greenbrier River. General Lee replaced him with General John Echols and ordered the unit back to Charleston, but a sizeable Federal army already occupied the city. The brigade returned to Narrows, Virginia, where it remained for the winter of 1862-1863.

In March 1863, Colonel Wharton received orders from General Samuel Jones, commanding the Department of Western Virginia, to place his brigade where it could defend the lead mines, the salt wells, and the Virginia and Tennessee Railroad in southwest Virginia. He established headquarters at Glade Springs, Virginia. His command of 1,154 men included the 51st and 50th Virginia Regiments, the 30th Virginia Battalion of Infantry, and Stamp's Artillery.

In June 1863, the 51st moved into Tennessee to support General Buckner's forces near Chattanooga where an expected attack did not appear. After two weeks, the regiment returned to Glade Springs. On June 27, Confederate cavalry drove away a Federal force at Saltville. Colonel Wharton reported that the 51st had 972 men.

After taking the train to Staunton, the troops marched to Woodstock and joined the Army of Northern Virginia under General Robert E. Lee on his march away from Gettysburg. On July 8, Wharton received a promotion to Brigadier General and Forsberg to Colonel of the 51st.

David Peirce Graham was at the White Sulphur Springs in present-day West Virginia in February 1863 acting as Commandant of the Post. He received a promotion to Major on July 8, 1863, thus becoming Major David Graham and giving his home in Wythe County the name most know it, by Major Graham's Mansion.

Early in August, General Lee ordered Wharton's Brigade to Warm Springs to block Federal General Averell's advance. Averell backed off and returned to West Virginia. During the summer of 1863, the 51st marched from Staunton to Glade Springs via Winchester, Orange Courthouse, Warm Springs, Dublin Depot, Abingdon, and Jonesboro, Tennessee.

Near the end of August, the brigade returned to southwest Virginia as the Federals made a determined effort to destroy the salt works, the lead mines, and the railroad. They captured Bristol and burned the town. The Confederates gathered all the forces they could get to oppose the Federals. At the last minute, the Union forces under General Burnside gave up the effort and returned to Knoxville. The Confederates pursued as far as Jonesboro, Tennessee.

General Robert Ransom assumed command of the Department of Western Virginia and Eastern Tennessee. He moved Wharton's Brigade to Blountville, Tennessee, to support General Longstreet who was trying to recapture Knoxville. All during the autumn of 1863, the 51st marched and counter-marched in the Rogersville-Bean Station area of Tennessee between the Holston River and the Clinch Mountains, expecting contact with the enemy at all times but seeing little fighting.

In January 1864, the 51st marched in General Longstreet's failed attempt to trap a Federal force near Dandridge, Tennessee. Many of the men had no shoes, and their bleeding feet left red marks in the snow. The men spent much time foraging during the bitterly cold winter, for in addition to food, they lacked clothing and shelter. The harsh winter took the lives of some soldiers. In one month, the strength of Wharton's Brigade (including the 51st and 45th Regiments and 30th Battalion of Infantry) dropped from 915 to 725 men.

The brigade, barely at the strength of a regiment, moved to Bull's Gap to protect the headquarters of the Department of East Tennessee in February. They repaired roads and performed picket duty. They had not seen battle in over a year.

In April 1864, the regiment marched to Abingdon in terrible weather over the muddiest possible roads. Woolwine presided over the execution of a deserter, writing, "the regiment being formed in two battalions to march out to the execution of John H. Jones of 30th Battalion Sharp Shooters of Grayson County for desertion. He was executed at two o'clock p.m."

On April 23, 1864, Major David Peirce Graham resigned his position due to health reasons. His service in the 51st Virginia was not stellar, but he lasted longer than most, and like many, the war broke his health at least temporarily.

The regiment fought on at New Market in May 1864 and with Jubal Early's Raid on Washington. Many were captured and sent to Fort Delaware until the end of the war.

On December 6, 1900, an aging man from Sweden rose to speak to the Garland Rodes Camp of the United Confederate Veterans in Lynchburg. Augustus Forsberg said, "Many years have passed since the events I have just narrated, and, like similar details of warfare, not of such importance as to merit a place in history, they will soon be forgotten. But the participants in the struggle of those 'days that tried men's souls' cannot readily forget the trials and perils to which they were exposed."

A few years ago, Tony Horowitz wrote a study of the Civil War titled *Confederates in the Attic,* a reference to having Southerners in your family tree. Little did he know the Graham Mansion already had Confederates or their spirits still meeting in the attic.

One investigator reported the following. "I remember on July 2, 2011, after a reenactment, the activity in the mansion was particularly stir crazy that night. It seemed that we had stirred up the war feelings. A member of a paranormal group seemed to think he was actually physically attacked with what felt like someone's hands going around his ankle and trying to hurt him. He was pretty shook up for a bit."

Major David Graham

62

Chapter Nine

Ghost Hunters

"There are two bodies — the rudimental and the complete; corresponding with the two conditions of the worm and the butterfly. What we call "death," is but the painful metamorphosis. Our present incarnation is progressive, preparatory, temporary. Our future is perfected, ultimate, immortal. The ultimate life is the full design."

Plumbers by day and paranormal investigators by night Jason Hawes and Grant Wilson of Rhode Island founded The Atlantic Paranormal Society (TAPS). Today, they are part of the most watched paranormal program on television SyFy Channel's Ghost Hunters. This one-hour weekly reality show comes from the creator and executive producer of *American Chopper*, Tom Thayer and Craig Piligian of Pilgrim Films.

In December 2011, TAPS and Ghost Hunters came to the Graham Mansion. The results of the visit aired in episode #805 on February 12, 2012, titled *Moonshine and Madness.*

Some of the subjects for investigation were a seven foot tall grey figure near the slave quarters seen from the road by passing motorists. The dining room had a moving chair and a stuffed animal falling off the wall when spirits were provoked. Another was a woman in a rocking chair on the second floor and another in the Confederate Room dressed in white. In "Clara's Room," there were sounds of dollhouse moving while a book was read. Other investigators heard giggling and a child's voice.

Downstairs in the shackle room, there were reports of people being touched and voices saying "Help Me." This author even heard his own name once during an investigation. Outside investigators heard whistling near the slave quarters that might have been coyotes.

The Ghost Hunters team took great care to debunk many things in the mansion such as in the basement the visitors being touched was dismissed due to the cobwebs, low ceilings and the pipes giving people the feeling of being touched. Provoking in the dining room resulted in no reaction from any spirits. Last, they test driving by the mansion while another investigator stood on the hill near the slave quarters with a flashlight making him appear a foot taller than his real height. The investigation led the Ghost Hunters team to an inconclusive opinion as to whether the Graham Mansion was haunted or not.

Jason Hawes, Josiah Weaver, Mary Linn Brewer, and Grant Wilson.

J. E. B. Stuart visited the Graham Mansion in the 1850s.

Chapter Ten

"Who You Gonna Call?"

"There is an eloquence in true enthusiasm"

The Graham Mansion is a house with disembodied voices, a place where people are touched when no one is there to feel them, where people see apparitions, where objects moving on their own, and even the smell of pipe smoke is present when no one is smoking.

The old idiom is "If you want something done right, do it yourself." Having participated in several paranormal investigations for this book, I am reminded of the old military saying, "Hurry up and wait." This chapter deals with the equipment one needs to be a proper paranormal investigator. Most of the results of such an investigation are not apparent at the time, but the use of this equipment allows you to find images and voices recorded during the event that give new insights to paranormal experiences.

EMF Detector

An Electro Magnetic Frequency Detector searches for energy fluctuations. A compass will spin when encountering

EMFs, but with an electronic device, the readings can be evaluated more consistently. A man made EMF will be constant while an inconsistent reading could be a spirit. Many people encounter cold spots as a sign of a spirit being present, and the idea is that a spirit uses energy to communicate.

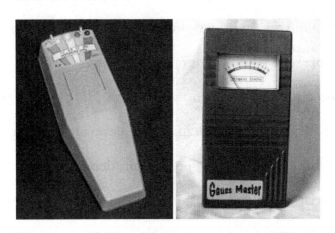

Thermal Imaging Camera

These cameras are used to see fluctuations in the heat signatures such as cold and hot spots or drafts. The presence of a heat signature is left when someone gets up out of a chair, for instance, leaving a residue that the camera detects and records.

Infrared Camera and Digital Video Recorder

The advent of digital technology allows paranormal investigators to avoid the days of replacing videotape every few hours. DVR provides monitoring, and digital recording video feeds from multiple cameras. Infrared allows night vision recording, and through wireless or wiring the central location for monitoring is now available.

Portable Tape Recorder

The portable tape or digital recorder is used to collect Electronic Voice Phenomena (EVP). Many investigators will ask questions and not hear a response with their own sense of hearing, but a recorder will and provide a record of the investigation. With the digital revolution in technology, an external microphone will improve the quality of the recording as much as ten times. The old days of analog tape with the noise of the tape are over.

Digital Thermometer

A thermometer needs to measure the surface temperatures, but more importantly for the paranormal investigator the ambient temperature or the temperature of the surroundings such as the atmosphere not the temperature of a wall or a table. A digital thermometer often detects cold spots indicating the presence of a spirit when the range might drop from ten to forty degrees in change.

Digital Video Camera

A camera can be carried by an investigator or placed in a stationary spot on a tripod. Adding an infrared illuminator will give the camera improvement in night vision as the standard model's record of poor quality. The ability to see in pitch-black darkness is vital for detecting events during an investigation.

Wireless Microphone

The ability to record audio to a central receiver and the software on a computer to receive and record input is vital to a paranormal investigation. While expensive setups abound today, many investigators still use baby monitors to hear, but the quality is not as good as a digital system.

Ion Generator

Many believe that spirits need the energy to reveal themselves. It is well noted during investigations that camera batteries will drain. An Ion Generator sends positive electrical charges into the atmosphere so that spirits can use the energy to communicate. An expert should make these devices as the possibility of electrocution is possible if not made or handled correctly.

White Noise Generator

Another device to be built by an expert in the field is

a White Noise Generator. Many feel that static white noise

is a catalyst for collecting EVPs. Others use the steady

constant noise for a baseline for EVPs.

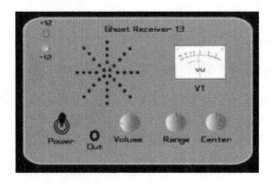

Afterword

The Last Word

"Convinced myself, I seek not to convince."

After a year with the Ghosts of the Graham Mansion, I am not sure that I believe the house is haunted or that paranormal activity is real, but I do think there are whole groups of people who are passionate about their beliefs in ghosts. It would be pure ignorance on my part to question what I do not have the senses to understand as I have seen people who do sense paranormal activity and believe strongly in these occurrences.

There is little doubt that the Graham Mansion is an eerie place to visit on a sunny, cloudless day and on a dark, foggy night, it is unbelievable in weirdness as any empty nearly two-hundred-year-old house should be. My only experience in the house was while scanning photos for The Graham Mansion: A History and Guide while sitting in the room to the left as you enter the front door. Out of the corner of my eye, I kept seeing something white and fluttering, but when I looked up, there was nothing or no one there. Was this a ghost or was my imagination set in motion by the stories heard about the house being haunted? I do not know, but this book is not meant to be the answer to the question. It is merely a book about the Ghosts of the Graham Mansion.

Glossary

"With me poetry has not been a purpose, but a passion."

Apparition: An unexpected sighting of a dead person.

Ascension: When one's energy evolves into a high form.

Clairscent: The smell of a scent from the spiritual world.

Clairvoyance: The ability to see spiritual people, animals, or object from another plane of existence.

Direct Voice Phenomena DVP: When someone from the spirit world communicates directly in their own voice.

Electronic Manipulation: When a spirit makes electronic equipment such as lights or televisions turn on and off.

Electronic Voice Phenomena EVP: Recording the voices of spirits and exist in the spirit world.

Ghost: A spirit that passed on, but stays in the physical world.

Haunting: The regular reappearance of an apparition at the same location or to the same individual.

Incarnation: When a spirit manifests itself into a physical room.

Intuition: When a person has the ability to know or understand things without conscious reasoning.

Karma: The belief that the good or a bad a person does in life will return to that person in the future. "What goes around comes around."

Medium: An intermediary who communicates between the physical and spiritual worlds.

Near Death Experience NDE: When the soul of a person who is clinically dead leaves their physical body, travels to the spiritual world, and then returns to their body.

Orbs: Appearing as small spheres in photographs and rarely outside them, they are white or translucent balls of energy.

Out of Body Experience OBE: The sensation of floating outside of one's body or perceiving one's body from a place outside it.

Physical World: Believed to be a manifestation of the spiritual world, it is where we human beings reside.

Psychic: A person that picks up impressions or reacts to psychic energy such as seeing images or hearing voices.

Reincarnation: Believing that one lived before in another lifetime.

Senses: The five human senses are sight, smell, taste, touch, and hearing. In the afterlife, souls have the other abilities such as the ability to see into the soul of a living thing and the ability to communicate with them.

Shadow People: Beings that appear as black silhouettes resembling human forms.

Signs: Communicating with those in the spiritual world to the physical world often in the form of objects used by loved ones who have passed.

Soul: The immaterial part of the individual or the individual part of a human that lives on after the death of the physical body.

Spirit: The part of the individual that lasts through eternity. Known as the "breath" from the Latin word spiritus, some people use the word spirit and ghost interchangeably.

Spirit World: The natural world of spirits and spiritual beings separate from the physical world of human beings where souls exist after death.

Telepathy: The ability to communicate from one mind to another.

Bibliography

Manuscript Collections
Graham Papers, University of Virginia
Reid S. Fulton Papers, Virginia Tech
Thomas D. Perry Papers, Virginia Tech

Private Collections
Papers of Mary Lin Brewer and Josiah C. Weaver

Government
1820 U. S. Census For Wythe County, Series M33   Roll #139
U. S. Census Agricultural Schedules, 1860, 1870,   1880, 1890

Books
Briggs, Constance Victoria. *Encyclopedia of the Unseen World.* San Francisco, 2010.
Fried, Sarah. *Constructing the Self: Female Identity Development in the   Turn of the Century South.* Vanderbilt University, Nashville, 2002.
Ingles, Anne. *Journal of Bettie Ann Graham.* New York, 1978.
Kegley, Mary B.
> *Early Adventures on the Western Waters, Volume III, Part 2.* Wytheville, 2004.
> *Glimpses of Wythe County, Virginia.* Wytheville, 1986.
> *Glimpses of Wythe County, Virginia, Volume Two.* Wytheville, 1988.
> *Wythe County, Virginia: A Bicentennial History.* Wytheville, 1989.

Presgraves, James S. *Wythe County Chapters.* Wytheville, 1972.
Taylor, Jr., L. B. *The Ghosts of Virginia. Volume 7, Chapter 47, pp 266-269. 2002.*
Tennis, Joe. *Haunts of Virginia's Blue Ridge Highlands.* Charleston SC, 2010.
Wythe County Historical Review
> No. 16, July 1979, pp 1-9
> No. 53, January 1998, pp. 11-18

Websites
Major Graham's Mansion http://majorgrahammansion.com

August Forsberg Diary
http://miley.wlu.edu/forsberg/transcript.html

Graham Genealogy
freepages.genealogy.rootsweb.ancestry.com/~walker/graham

Paranormal Groups

Black Diamond http://blackdiamondps.org

Haunted South http://www.hauntedsouthtv.com

Mountain Ridge

http://www.mountainridgeparanormalresearchsociety.com

Paranormal West Virginia http://www.paranormalwv.webs.com

Proof Positive http://www.proofpositiveparanormal.com

Ghost Hunters

http://www.syfy.com/ghosthunters/episodes/season/8/episode/805/moonshine_madness

Newspapers and Magazines
Big Blue Summer/Fall 2009
Bristol Herald Courier: August 28, 2008;
Christiansburg News Messenger: November 14,   2007;
Des Moines, Iowa, Evening Tribune: July 13, 1921;
Des Moines, Iowa, Register: August 30, 1921;
Drake University Delphic: March 4, 1921;
Newsweek: August 12, 1963;
North Pinellas Times: July 30, 2006;
Richmond Times Dispatch: July 16, 1978;
Roanoke Times and World News: November 14, 1954;
March 5, 1978; October 28, 2007;
Southwest Enterprise: January 13, 1974; March 14, 1978;
August 13, 1981; January 4, 1997; July 4, 2006; August
30, 2007;
St. Petersburg (FL) Times: July 20, 2006;
Sunday Times Journal: November 14, 1976;

About The Author

J. E. B. Stuart's biographer, Emory Thomas, describes Tom Perry as "a fine and generous gentleman who grew up near Laurel Hill, where Stuart grew up, has founded J. E. B. Stuart Birthplace, and attracted considerable interest in the preservation of Laurel Hill. He has started a symposium series about aspects of Stuart's life to sustain interest in Stuart beyond Ararat, Virginia." Perry graduated from Patrick County High School in 1979 and Virginia Tech in 1983 with a bachelor's degree in history.

Tom founded the J. E. B. Stuart Birthplace in 1990. The non-profit organization has preserved 75 acres of the Stuart property including the house site where J. E. B. Stuart was born on February 6, 1833. Perry wrote the eight interpretive signs about Laurel Hill's history along with the Virginia Civil War Trails sign and the new Virginia Historical Highway Marker in 2002. He spent many years researching and traveling all over the nation to find Stuart materials. He continues his work to preserve Stuart's Birthplace, producing the Laurel Hill Teacher's Guide for educators and the Laurel Hill Reference Guide for groups.

Perry can be seen on Virginia Public Television's Forgotten Battlefields: The Civil War in Southwest Virginia, with his mentor, noted Civil War Historian Dr. James I. Robertson, Jr. Perry has begun a collection of papers relating to Stuart and Patrick County history in the Special Collections Department of the Carol M. Newman Library at Virginia Tech under the auspices of the Virginia Center for Civil War Studies.

Historian Thomas D. Perry is the author and publisher of over forty books on regional history in Virginia surrounding his home county of Patrick. He is the author of ten books on Patrick County, Virginia, including Ascent to Glory, The Genealogy of J. E. B. Stuart, The Free State of Patrick: Patrick County Virginia in the Civil War, The Dear Old Hills of Patrick: J. E. B. Stuart and Patrick County, Virginia, Images of America: Patrick County Virginia, and Notes From The Free State Of Patrick.

For a decade, Perry taught Civil War history to every eleventh-grade history class at his alma mater, Patrick County High School, from his book The Free State of Patrick: Patrick County Virginia in the Civil War. He can be seen on Henrico County Virginia's DVD documentary Bold Dragoon: The Life of J. E. B. Stuart.

http://henrico-va.granicus.com/MediaPlayer.php?clip_id=1088

Perry was a featured presenter at the Virginia Festival of the Book in 2012. He speaks all over the country on topics as far ranging as Andy Griffith to J. E. B. Stuart.

In 2004, Perry began The Free State of Patrick Internet History Group, which became the largest historical organization in the area, with over 500 members. It covered Patrick County,

Virginia, and regional history. Tom produced a monthly email newsletter about regional history entitled Notes From The Free State of Patrick that comes from his website, www.freestateofpatrick.com.

In 2009, Perry used his book Images of America Henry County Virginia to raise over $25,000 for the Bassett Historical Center, "The Best Little Library in Virginia," and as editor of the Henry County Heritage Book raised another $30,000. Perry was responsible for over $200,000 of the $800,000 raised to expand the regional history library.

He is the recipient of the John E. Divine Award from the Civil War Education Association, the Hester Jackson Award from the Surry County Civil War Round Table, and the Best Article Award from the Society of North Carolina Historians for his article on Stoneman's Raid in 2008. In 2010, he received acknowledgment from the Bassett Public Library Association for his work to expand the Bassett Historical Center and was named Henry County Virginia Man of the Year by www.myhenrycounty.com. The Sons of the American Revolution presented Tom with the Good Citizenship Award. Perry also recently received the National Society of the Daughters of the American Revolution Community Service Award from the Patrick Henry Daughters of the American Revolution.

Perry has remembered the history of those who helped him. He worked with the Virginia Department of Transportation to name the bridge over the Dan River after his neighbor, Command Sergeant Major Zeb Stuart Scales, who was the most decorated non-commissioned soldier from Patrick County, Virginia. Perry remembered his teachers at Blue Ridge Elementary School including his father, Erie Perry, who was a teacher and principal for thirty years in The Free State of Patrick, by placing a monument to the retired teachers at the school in Ararat, Virginia.

Perry, a recognized authority on J. E. B. Stuart is presently working on a three volume projected titled The Papers of J. E. B. Stuart.

Made in the USA
Middletown, DE
05 April 2023

27916430R00050